CRIME SCIENCE

SPY STALKERS

Using Science to Catch Spies

CHERITON
CHILDREN'S BOOKS

Published in 2023 by **Cheriton Children's Books**
1 Bank Drive West, Shrewsbury, Shropshire, SY3 9DJ, UK

© 2023 Cheriton Children's Books

First Edition

Author: Sarah Eason
Designer: Paul Myerscough
Editor: Louisa Simmons
Proofreader: Ella Hammond

Printed in China

Please visit our website,
www.cheritonchildrensbooks.com
to see more of our high-quality books.

CONTENTS

CHAPTER 1

STALKING A SPY

Movies and television dramas often feature spy stories, and most of us love to watch them, but in real life, spying is a serious problem. Today, the world is full of spies who pose a very real threat to the **security** of countries and businesses. When people talk about spying, they often refer to it as espionage. This describes any activities that involve gaining sensitive or **confidential** information about another person, organization, or country without **permission**—and, ideally, without them ever knowing.

The Dangers of Spying

At the very least, spying is an invasion of another person's privacy. At worst, it can threaten the safety and **stability** of a country, and even the world. Every day, espionage on top-secret government, military, and business data takes place. It can cost billions and cause devastating disruption. For that reason, stalking spies is important work, and highly trained people spend their days doing just that.

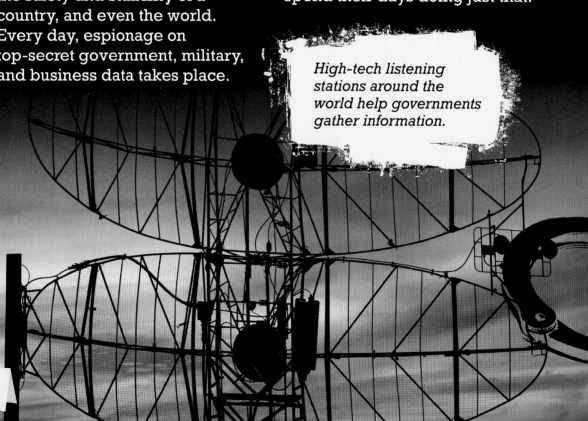

High-tech listening stations around the world help governments gather information.

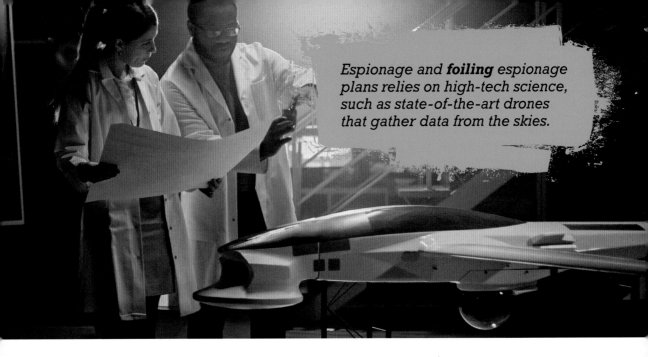

*Espionage and **foiling** espionage plans relies on high-tech science, such as state-of-the-art drones that gather data from the skies.*

The Science of Spying

The essence of all espionage, whether it be spying or **monitoring** a spy, is gathering information. To do this, many governments use undercover spies—or secret agents, as they are popularly known. However, unlike in the movies, most espionage work is carried out by people in offices. To do their job, they rely on **intelligence**-gathering technology based on the latest cutting-edge science. This could be powerful **radar** listening stations, Internet-monitoring technology, or video cameras attached to **satellites** positioned high above Earth. Much of this technology was originally developed for the army, navy, and air force.

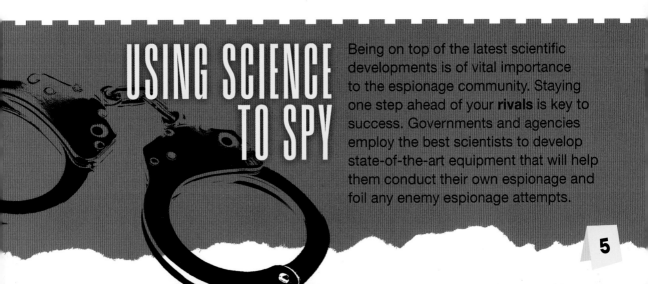

USING SCIENCE TO SPY

Being on top of the latest scientific developments is of vital importance to the espionage community. Staying one step ahead of your **rivals** is key to success. Governments and agencies employ the best scientists to develop state-of-the-art equipment that will help them conduct their own espionage and foil any enemy espionage attempts.

Crossing Lines

Stalking spies blurs the boundaries between what is **legal** and **illegal**, in pursuit of information that could help prevent crime, **terrorism**, and war. Espionage work is undertaken by a wide range of people, from undercover spies to agents in office buildings. Some spies are positioned in overseas **embassies**, while others are issued with convincing cover stories, for example, they may pose as regular businesspeople.

Secret Agents

The main job of a secret agent is to go out and gather information about the activities of foreign governments. The United States' secret service is called the National Clandestine Service (NCS), and is operated by the Central Intelligence Agency (CIA). Other countries have similar organizations, for example, the British equivalent of the CIA is known as MI6, or the Secret Intelligence Service (SIS).

Government offices overseas, known as embassies, hide spies and secret agents.

TRUE SPY STORY

Espionage is a dangerous world, and never more so than when a spy turns against their own country to help another. In 2021, three former intelligence **operatives** from the United States admitted to working for the United Arab Emirates' (UAE) DarkMatter computer security company. The operatives **hacked** US computers and electronic devices to gain information for DarkMatter. US intelligence sources believe the information was used by the UAE government. The operatives, Daniel Gericke, Ryan Adams, and Marc Baier, helped DarkMatter use advanced cybertechnology to direct attacks at enemies and political rivals within the United States.

Spies are trained to blend in with everyday people, and their covers are convincing.

Secret Gadgets

In movies, spies are rarely without high-tech gadgets. While most of the tools shown are the work of imagination, it is true that secret agents are often provided with ingenious gadgets. Over the years, these have included pens that write with invisible ink, hollowed-out books that hide USB memory sticks, and tiny radio transmitters.

BUILD AN ARMY

The secret service headquarters of the most powerful countries in the world house an army of staff. The United States, Russia, and China have some of the world's biggest spy networks. For the people who work within them, their job is to carry out routine surveillance to uncover any threat to their country's security.

Daily Tasks

Most secret agents have quite uneventful jobs. Some are employed to monitor emails sent by suspected spies, listen to secret messages picked up by government listening stations, or communicate with agents based around the world. Other agents are responsible for gathering all known information about a particular subject, such as attempts by **rogue** countries to build dangerous nuclear weapons. Some agents are responsible for keeping their country's president briefed about top-secret information.

Double Agents

To become a secret agent, people must pass vigorous security checks. This is to make sure that they are not likely to pass on information to the secret services of other nations. Over the years, many spies have been exposed as "double agents." These are agents who are employed by one agency, such as the CIA, but are secretly working for another. Double agents pose a huge risk because they often have access to highly sensitive information about national security.

Spy Science

The CIA has secretly spent many millions of dollars creating scientific conferences around the world. The aim of them is to draw in scientists from countries that may pose a threat to the United States. At the conference settings, agents can gather intelligence from foreign scientists about possible nuclear or **biological warfare** plans in their countries, which can then be used to better protect the United States.

Gatherings such as science conventions and conferences are events in which useful intelligence about technological developments around the world can be compiled.

Billionaire Spies

Often, people believe that only governments carry out espionage. That's not true. Today, spying is big business—it is increasingly seen in the business world as companies try to get the edge on their competitors. That type of spying is called industrial espionage, and it can cost many businesses billions of dollars.

War planes based on top-secret US technology may have been built by countries that pose a threat to the United States.

Big-Business Secrets

The world of business is highly competitive, and some companies will stop at nothing to get ahead of their rivals. Industrial espionage is illegal because it usually involves stealing lists of customers, plans for new products, or information regarding the science behind cutting-edge technology. If a company can get hold of this type of information about its rivals, it may be able to use it to make similar products, or gain some other competitive advantage. For example, if a rival computer company stole detailed plans for a new iPhone, Apple could potentially lose billions of dollars.

SPY SCIENCE

Electromagnetic shielding is a technique used to cut down on industrial espionage. Electrical equipment **emits** what is known as electrical radiation. This is waves of invisible energy.

Electrical radiation can sometimes give away vital information. Electromagnetic shielding is a tool that stops electrical radiation, ensuring no sensitive information seeps out.

Not Just Businesses

Some governments also take part in industrial espionage in order to steal or copy technology that they have not yet developed themselves. For example, it is thought that the Chinese Chengdu J-20 stealth fighter jet is based on a US F-117 Nighthawk plane. After an F-117 crashed in Serbia, it was reported that Chinese officials bought the remaining parts, which were then very carefully studied. Eventually, the Chinese were able to design a new jet fighter with alarming similarities to the F-117.

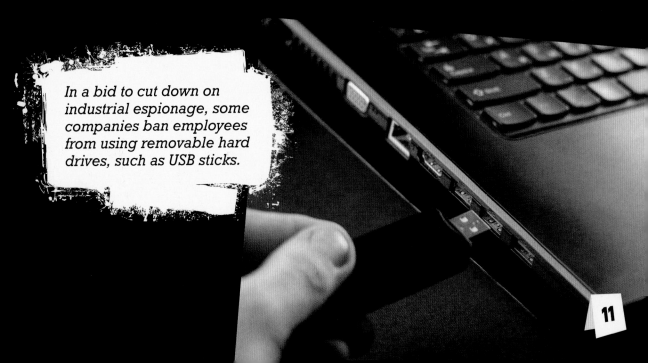

In a bid to cut down on industrial espionage, some companies ban employees from using removable hard drives, such as USB sticks.

CHAPTER 2

SPIES AND EARS

Surveillance is all-important in missions to capture enemy secret agents. Surveillance describes all activities that involve watching, listening, or monitoring. The secret services use a wide variety of surveillance techniques. They include "human intelligence" (things seen or heard by agents or informants), undercover filming, **intercepting** electronic communications, and secretly recording telephone conversations.

Satellites That Spy

Finding out what enemy spies are reporting on is crucial in the first line of defense against espionage in **hostile** countries. Over the years, the US government has launched a number of spy satellites that were specifically designed to intercept Russian and Chinese communications. These listening satellites in space feature massive dishes, which reflect communications signals back toward Earth.

Covertly, or secretly, watching somebody's movements is a basic form of surveillance.

Secret and Scrambled

Intercepting messages is one thing, but understanding them is another. Most top-secret messages are encrypted, which means they are scrambled in some way, or sent in a secret code. Even if these messages cannot be understood, there is still value in monitoring them. That is because knowing who is sending and receiving messages, and how often, is almost as valuable as knowing what the message says. For example, it would be useful to know if two enemy states communicate regularly because it would suggest some type of working relationship.

SPY SCIENCE

A lot of secret communications are sent around the world using very short radio waves called microwaves. Although they are sent between top-secret sites using radar technology, some of the microwaves drift up into space. Some spy satellites have been designed to help intercept these messages by **deflecting** the signals back toward radar listening stations on Earth.

Tiny Spies

Police forces now use surveillance techniques originally developed by the espionage community. It is not uncommon for police to record phone calls from **suspects,** or to place covert recording devices, known as bugs, in suspects' homes. Bugs contain both a microphone and a tiny radio transmitter. When the device is switched on, it is possible to listen to private conversations many miles away.

Smart Spying

Spies also use tiny body-worn hidden cameras to film their subjects and transmit the images taken back to their headquarters. The devices can be disguised as ordinary modern-day technology or accessories, even including smartwatches and sunglasses.

Location services on smartphones and satellite navigation in vehicles are based on technology originally created for spying.

TRUE SPY STORY

In the 1970s, Russian secret agents posing as laborers managed to plant hundreds of listening devices inside the walls of the US Embassy in Moscow. The US government eventually found so many bugs that the building had to be demolished and built again from scratch!

Out-Spying Spies

Spies also use countersurveillance technology to make sure they, themselves, are not being spied on. Tiny devices can scan an area for bugs and other surveillance devices, alerting the spy to any espionage tools or activity nearby.

From Secret to Useful

Over the last 100 years, amazing espionage science has led to the invention of many incredible new and game-changing technologies. And technology that originally started out as top secret has sometimes become a tool that ordinary people use. For example, satellite navigation or location services on smartphones began life as military surveillance technologies, but are now tools used by many people.

To avoid detection, bugs are usually small enough to easily be hidden inside other ordinary objects.

Radar for Spying

Most modern surveillance technology has been built around a system called radar, which sends and receives waves of energy called radio waves. Radar systems can be used in many different ways, from helping planes reach their destinations to listening out for covert messages from spies.

War Weapon

Radar systems were first used during World War II (1939–1945). Since that time, radar has been developed for use in many different fields. Radar systems are used by weather forecasters to detect storms. Radar is also used to communicate with satellites high above Earth, and also by submarines to figure out their exact location. Over the years, the US government has spent billions of dollars building radar stations in places all over the world. They include Ascension Island in the Atlantic Ocean and Opana Hill in Hawaii.

How Do Radars Work?

Radar systems send and receive radio waves to figure out the exact location of objects, for example, airplanes or storm clouds. When radio waves sent from a radar transmitter hit an object, a certain amount will be deflected toward the transmitter. By measuring how long it takes for the deflected waves to return, radar systems can figure out where the object is.

Enormous radar dishes can be used to listen to secret communications, such as telephone calls, from many thousands of miles away.

QUIET

Dual Purpose

Radar stations have two main purposes.
The first is as an early-warning system
against possible attack from the air,
for example, by long-range missiles.
The second is to scour the world for
rogue communications that may be of
assistance to the espionage community.
The receivers used in radar stations are
incredibly powerful. Sometimes, they
look like enormous satellite dishes or
oversized golf balls. They are capable
of picking up stray radio transmissions
from many thousands of miles away.

*Radar systems were
first used to detect
any enemy aircraft
during World War II.*

Spy Satellites

Radar is not the only way that governments keep tabs on the activities of other nations. Many countries, including the United States, China, and Russia, also own and operate a network of secretive spy satellites that are positioned high above Earth.

Watching Over Us

Spy satellites are effectively powerful telescopes. Instead of pointing toward outer space, they are pointed toward Earth. They are used to film or take photographs of enemy military bases, power stations, and communications buildings.

Spy satellites can take detailed photographs of foreign military sites.

Sputnik and Corona

The first spy satellite, Sputnik, was launched by the Soviet Union in 1957. During the 1960s, the US government developed its own version, named Corona. Corona was used to take photos of Soviet missile sites. In more recent years, spy satellites have become far more powerful. They can now provide live film footage as well as photographs of their targets.

Satellites Kept Secret

The information we have regarding spy satellites is mostly outdated. It is not known how many US, Russian, or Chinese spy satellites are currently **orbiting** Earth. We also do not know exactly what the satellites are used for, although experts say that they are used just as much for intercepting communications as filming or taking photographs. On rare occasions, images taken by spy satellites will be shown to the public. This usually happens after successful military missions.

TRUE SPY STORY

In recent years, Chinese spy balloons have been spotted over the United States, and some have been shot down by US military aircraft. It is believed that the balloons have been used by the Chinese to gather intelligence about the United States.

Spy satellite imagery is used to help coordinate military operations.

Dangerous Drones

In addition to spy satellites and radar listening stations, some governments also use Unmanned Aerial Vehicles (UAVs), better known as drones. These unmanned planes can fly close to the action for a bird's-eye view of what is happening far below.

Controlled from the Ground

Drones are radio-controlled planes. A pilot sits in a room at a military base and controls the plane from there. Drones have a number of benefits over regular planes—they have the ability to fly much closer to the ground and because the planes are not piloted from within, if they are shot down, there is no risk of loss of life.

Armed and Unarmed

There are two main types of drones—those that carry weapons and are used by the military for remote attacks, and those that are unarmed. It is these unarmed drones that are used by the CIA and US military for espionage.

The US government uses unmanned drone planes to spy on suspected terrorists around the world.

Drones can carry out surveillance work both discreetly and quickly.

Drone Alert

There are numerous reports of unmanned drones being used to spy on military bases, according to security sources. In fact, hundreds of Chinese-manufactured drones have been seen in restricted airspace over Washington, D.C. The drones have been flown over no-go zones around the capital, and the concern is that they are gathering intelligence about government buildings and **personnel**. While the drones may not have been **commissioned** by the Chinese government, the concern is that the data they collect could be gathered and used in the future.

SPY SCIENCE

Unarmed drones are used almost exclusively for surveillance. The drones carry a number of different cameras for filming, including night vision. Night vision ensures good-quality pictures in the dark, something regular cameras cannot do. Pictures from drones are beamed live to government agents so that they can be **analyzed**.

JOIN A SPY CLUB

The Five Eyes (FVEY) is an alliance of countries that cooperate to gather intelligence. The joint partnership is between the governments of the United States, United Kingdom (UK), Canada, New Zealand, and Australia. The alliance began loosely during World War II, then became a more formal arrangement during the **Cold War**, in the 1960s. At that point, the alliance created the biggest surveillance network the world has ever seen. It is called ECHELON.

High-Tech Interception

ECHELON is thought to be able to intercept communications sent all over the world via satellite, telephone, microwaves, and the Internet.
One part of the system, called PRISM, collects information from technology organizations such as Google and Apple, while another part, called Upstream, gathers information from the communications of ordinary people, for example, by text, email, or telephone.

The ECHELON system is simple to understand. A large number of radar listening stations and other surveillance facilities around the world are joined together using secure, top-secret communication links. The information captured by each facility—be it microwave communications, emails, or phone calls—is shared between each of the five ECHELON nations for espionage purposes. The shared information is used to monitor espionage activities of countries and organizations that are seen as possible threats.

Room 641A

At least one Internet interception facility is being run by ECHELON. It is called Room 641A, and is based in San Francisco. It is situated at a site run by AT&T, through which flows a large proportion of the world's Internet traffic—such as emails, requests to access websites, and posts on social networking sites. It is likely that Room 641A is just one of a number of similar sites around the world run by ECHELON.

Split-Second Analysis

According to technicians who used to work at the AT&T site, the CIA installed a super-computer there called NarusInsight. The computer is able to capture and analyze huge amounts of information in just a matter of nanoseconds.

Many radar listening sites used as part of the ECHELON network feature buildings that look like giant golf balls.

23

CHAPTER 3
SPIES AND CODES

Governments know that spies or surveillance experts may intercept their top-secret messages, so many have developed ingenious secret codes or ways of hiding messages within other communications. This is known as cryptography.

During World War II, the Germans used a special typewriter called the Enigma Machine to send secret, coded messages to generals in the field.

Understanding Cryptography

Thousands of years ago, the first known cryptography was used in ancient Egypt to hide messages in symbols. Although cryptography is thousands of years old, the basic principles of the coding system have remained the same. The idea is to create a system for writing messages that can be understood only by a very small number of people, specifically those who have a set of instructions. These instructions are known as a key. The key sets out the details of the code used, be it numbers instead of letters, random letters, or a combination of both. But cryptography is not just about secret messages sent in code. Some organizations also use messages hidden in other objects—even embedded within digital photographs, for example.

Most Talented

Deciphering messages, which is effectively cracking secret codes, can be time-consuming and, on occasions, almost impossible to do. For that reason, those who develop or crack secret codes on behalf of governments are among the most talented mathematicians and scientists in the world.

TRUE SPY STORY

The outcome of World War II was hanging in the balance until British mathematicians cracked the Nazi's top-secret code. The Germans used Enigma to create code from scrambled letters and numbers. After scientist Bill Tutte cracked the code, the British were able to develop the world's first programmable computer to help decipher messages.

Bill Tutte and a team of code-breakers cracked the Enigma code using ingenious technology. Their work can be seen on display at Bletchley Park Museum, England, today.

The Shortwave Set

Communicating without arousing suspicion can be difficult, even for the most highly-skilled secret agents. One traditional method of communication that is still in use is broadcasting seemingly random sets of numbers by shortwave radio, called a one-way voice link.

One-Way Link

The one-way voice link system works as follows: At set times of the day, an unidentified voice reads out a set of numbers, in sequence, on a certain shortwave radio frequency. This system is known as a numbers station. In theory, anyone with a shortwave radio receiver can tune in, although nobody other than the spy being communicated with will be able to understand the message. The messages are written and deciphered using a one-time pad, which is said to be an unbreakable code system.

The KGB relied on technology to help them transmit carefully coded messages.

TRUE SPY STORY

The Russian secret police, known as the KGB, used one-time pads that were so tiny they could fit in the palm of a hand or even inside a walnut shell! Pads were also sometimes printed onto sheets of nitrocellulose, which easily catches fire. If the owner of the pad was concerned it could fall into enemy hands, it could be burned instantly.

One-Time Pad

The one-time pad relies on spies being issued with a series of numbered key sheets containing random sets of five letters. Copies of the key sheets are also held by the agents who write the numbers broadcasts.

Listening spies are told in advance, usually at the start of the broadcast, which numbered key sheet to use to decipher the message. The numbers read out in each broadcast seem random to untrained ears, but they actually represent different letters of the alphabet. Using basic math and the key sheet, the listening spy can easily figure out the message.

Hidden Messages

There are many ways to send secret messages. One of the best-known of methods is steganography: the science of hiding messages in letters or pictures. Steganography can take different forms including text, images, video, and sound.

Invisible Ink

Traditionally, the most common form of steganography is the use of invisible ink. Most invisible inks are developed using chemicals. To reveal the hidden message, the spy may have to gently heat the paper, rub another chemical over the paper, or hold it under a special type of light. To conceal messages written in invisible ink, most spies will hide them within a regular letter. The "invisible" part may be written in the spaces between each line of the letter.

Messages in Pictures

Today, computers are used to create hidden messages. One ingenious method is hiding messages inside digital pictures. These images are made up of hundreds of thousands of individual dots or square blocks, called pixels. By changing certain pixels, it is possible to send a message to someone. For example, each letter of the alphabet could be given a particular color. By changing every hundredth pixel to the color that corresponds to the letter of the alphabet, spies can conceal quite complicated messages.

Sensitive data hidden in code can provide intelligence agencies with critical information.

Keeping Secrets Secret

Steganography is very useful when sending classified information that could be dangerous in the wrong hands. It is often used to send sensitive information that could be used by spy agents working for hostile countries. Steganography is increasingly used by law enforcement agencies, the military, and intelligence agencies to pass sensitive information to colleagues.

This Microsoft logo, hidden inside a digital image in an instruction manual, is a good example of how photographs can be used to send messages.

SPY SCIENCE

There are now many steganography **software** programs that help people hide information. Forensic scientists are trained in the programs, and how they conceal data, so that they can search for it when looking for sensitive information such as communications between enemy intelligence agencies.

CRACK THE CODE

The computer age has increased the importance of cryptography not just in espionage, but also within our ordinary, day-to-day lives. The passwords we use to protect our home computers are one low-level example of cryptography in action.

Password Protection

With a little knowledge, most computer passwords are easy to crack. However, the same cannot be said about the data-encryption techniques used by governments and secret agents to make sure their electronic communications are protected from prying eyes. Governments employ specialists in computer security to create forms of data encryption that are almost impossible to decipher. They also employ cryptanalysts, whose job it is to find weaknesses in other computer security systems.

Cryptanalysts are usually computer scientists with a deep knowledge of math. As well as trying to find weaknesses in the computer systems used by other nations, they also test out the strength of their own government's systems. Some cryptanalysts take part in side-channel attacks, which are attempts to figure out the weaknesses in a security system by measuring the time it takes for a computer to perform a task, the amount of power used to perform a task, or the electrical radiation a computer emits.

Spy Science

A computer system that uses encrypted information to protect against hacking or send secret messages is known as a cryptosystem. An example is a secure email system, where messages can be sent and received only by two or more computers using the same encryption software. This software will encrypt, or scramble, the message when it is sent. Should the message fall into the wrong hands, it will not be understood.

It is the job of cryptanalysts to stop vital, top-secret information from falling into the hands of terrorists, which could result in devastating attacks.

CHAPTER 4

THE INFORMATION WAR

In the twenty-first century, many people believe that the greatest threat to our security does not come from traditional methods of espionage. Instead, it comes from those using advanced techniques to spy on us with computers. This is the world of cyberespionage.

Stalking the Internet

Cyberespionage is a growing problem. Most cyberespionage agents, or cyberspies, are experts in hacking. Hacking is the method of obtaining access to top-secret networks or breaking through security systems using specially created software. This **malicious** software, sometimes also called "malware," can be used to destroy computers, weaken security systems, and gain access to top-secret documents.

Cyberspies can steal information that is precious to both organizations and ordinary individuals.

Cyberattacks by foreign countries are a growing threat to the U.S. military. It is now employing many more specialized people to help deal with the attacks.

Spying Today

In recent years, the number of incidents of attempted cyberespionage has increased dramatically. The US government believes that certain nations are behind some of the attacks, secretly employing top hackers to steal state secrets such as nuclear missile codes and military plans.

Counterintelligence

The CIA handles a lot of the US government's cyberespionage work. The organization's Counterintelligence Center Analysis Group was first set up to identify and analyze the efforts of foreign intelligence agencies, which are secret-service organizations run by other countries. As well as monitoring traditional espionage activities, it now also handles cyberespionage.

SPY SCIENCE

One of the most dangerous pieces of software used by cyberspies is a Trojan horse. This is a piece of software that is hidden inside a seemingly normal email attachment, such as a picture.

When the recipient opens the attachment, the Trojan horse is installed. This allows the cyberspy to access the computer and steal important documents without the user's knowledge.

War by Computer

There is growing evidence that certain countries are deliberately setting out to hack into computers that belong to other nations not just to spy on them, but to also cause damage to the countries' systems. This has become known as cyberwarfare.

War on a New Front

The US government is so worried about the potential of cyberwarfare that it now classes the Internet as the "fifth theater of conflict"—the others are land, sea, air, and space. In recent years, the White House has announced that hackers, reportedly working for the Chinese government, had gained access to top-secret information, potentially including nuclear missile command codes. It is largely believed that this was achieved by using a Trojan horse.

Attack and Weaken

Cyberwarfare is the next step up from cyberespionage. Usually, cyberwarfare attacks are much larger and more persistent. They may come from many different sources at once, rather than a single computer or small network. Although they may have similar aims—for example, to steal government secrets—the aim of cyberwarfare is usually to weaken government "cyberdefenses."

SPY SCIENCE

Cyberspies and hackers regularly use a technique called keylogging to record details of what people are typing into their computers. Once a hacker has gained access to a computer using a Trojan horse, they can install malware that records every key the user presses. The hacker can then read secret emails or documents as they are being written.

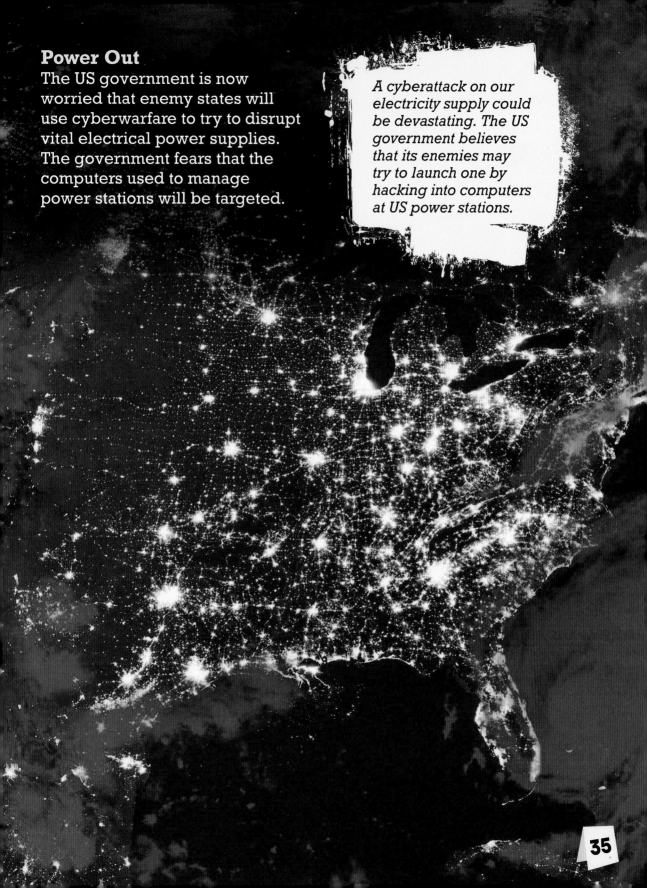

Power Out

The US government is now worried that enemy states will use cyberwarfare to try to disrupt vital electrical power supplies. The government fears that the computers used to manage power stations will be targeted.

A cyberattack on our electricity supply could be devastating. The US government believes that its enemies may try to launch one by hacking into computers at US power stations.

The Invisible Threat

Cyberspies go to great lengths to hide their identity. As a result, finding out who is behind large-scale cyberwarfare attacks can be difficult. However, a lot of the evidence points to two countries that have difficult relations with the West—Iran and China.

Battles with Iran

In the past, the US government has launched cyberattacks against Iran. In 2010, hackers working for the CIA attacked the computer systems at several Iranian nuclear power stations. The US government hoped that this would slow attempts by Iran to build nuclear weapons. In 2012, the computer systems of a number of Western oil companies were attacked in what the US government claims was an act by the government of Iran. Over the years that followed, an increasing number of cyberattacks were launched by both countries, and from 2020 onward the United States acknowledged that it was engaged in an ongoing **virtual** battle with Iran.

The US government launched cyberattacks on Iranian power plants to try and prevent the country advancing its nuclear weapons program.

TRUE SPY STORY

By far the most successful cyberespionage research project to date is InfoWar Monitor, which was funded by Canadian universities and technology companies. Its scientists traced the origins of a large-scale cyberspying operation codenamed GhostNet, which attacked computers in government buildings around the world using a Trojan horse called Ghost Rat. This enabled GhostNet hackers to take control of government computers and steal top-secret information.

Using highly advanced techniques, including forensic computer analysis and laboratory testing, InfoWar Monitor traced the source of the attacks to Hainan Island, China, home of a Chinese secret-service facility.

Gifted university students are helping to track down cyberspies.

Chinese Whispers

In the past, China lagged behind some Western countries in industries such as science, technology, and the manufacturing of weapons. Because of this, Chinese hackers targeted the computer systems of US companies. Their aim was to steal information that could help them develop their own rival software, gadgets, or weapons. In recent years, however, China has begun to lead the way in technological developments, and has targeted the US government more closely in hacking attempts.

COVID–19 Attack

The US government also believes the United States was a victim of Chinese hacking during the COVID-19 **pandemic**, when it is alleged that hackers linked to the Chinese government stole more than $20 million in US COVID relief benefits that were intended to help small businesses and citizens during the pandemic. US secret service agents believe that the hackers stole money across all 50 states of the United States.

Science Super-Spying

The issue of cyberspies hacking into government computer systems is not the only area of concern. It is also possible for secret agents to gain access to information from computers, using advanced scientific techniques.

Dangerous Radiation

All electrical equipment gives off invisible waves of energy, called radiation. According to a scientist named Wim van Eck, it is possible to read any data displayed on a computer screen, or typed into a computer keyboard, if you have the technology to capture and analyze that computer's electrical radiation. He calls this technique of secretly "eavesdropping" on electrical radiation "Van Eck Phreaking." This is just one of the techniques that make it possible, although still difficult, to gain vital information and state secrets by recording and analyzing radiation.

TEMPEST Testing

To counter the problem of electrical eavesdropping, the US government joined forces with other countries to create a program called TEMPEST.

Today, computers used by the secret services are designed to emit less electromagnetic radiation.

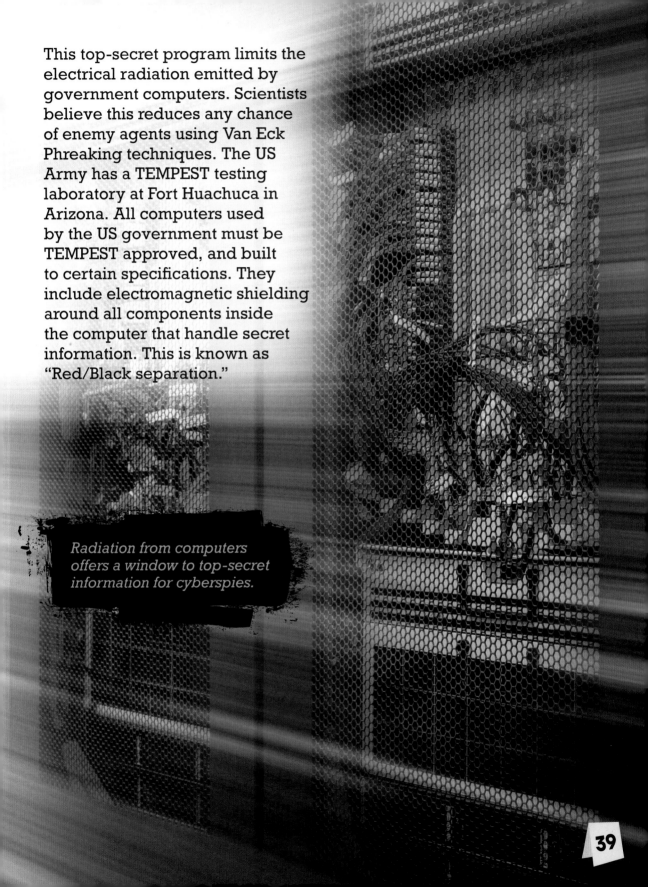

This top-secret program limits the electrical radiation emitted by government computers. Scientists believe this reduces any chance of enemy agents using Van Eck Phreaking techniques. The US Army has a TEMPEST testing laboratory at Fort Huachuca in Arizona. All computers used by the US government must be TEMPEST approved, and built to certain specifications. They include electromagnetic shielding around all components inside the computer that handle secret information. This is known as "Red/Black separation."

Radiation from computers offers a window to top-secret information for cyberspies.

DEFEND YOUR COUNTRY

Given the enormous increase in cyberespionage attacks in recent decades, it is no surprise that the US government takes the information war very seriously. That is why the government set up a new department of the armed forces: CYBERCOM.

Stop Attacks

Short for Cyber Command, CYBERCOM is based at Fort Meade, in Maryland. CYBERCOM features representatives from the computer technology departments of all the major armed forces. Its role is to defend US government computer networks against cyberattacks and cyberespionage.

Hit Back

CYBERCOM is also charged with carrying out any aggressive cyberattacks against other nations ordered by the president.

CYBERCOM was the world's first cyberwarfare organization. It also built the world's very first Cyberwarfare Intelligence Center, a type of cyberespionage headquarters, at Lackland Air Force Base in Texas.

Spy Science

It is thought that CYBERCOM agents divide their time between rigorously testing military computer systems, developing new methods to combat the cyberwarfare threat, and launching secret cyberattacks against enemy nations. In 2022, the department also turned its attention to helping stop malicious cyberattacks against Ukraine by Russian agents. The information gathered by the department is now being used to also better defend the United States against future cyberattacks.

While under the leadership of Vladimir Putin, Russia is believed to have ordered a number of cyberattacks against Ukraine as well as carrying out physical attacks against the country.

THE FUTURE OF ESPIONAGE

The methods used by spies and secret agents may have changed over the last 50 years, but espionage remains a huge problem for governments and businesses around the world, and the threat from cyberespionage will continue to rapidly grow.

The Science of Spying

Both science and technology play a huge role in espionage. Over the years, competing nations have been involved in a scientific arms race to develop new forms of surveillance technology. All major nations, wherever they are based in the world, have their own secret intelligence operations. Some are bigger than others, but all have the same aim: to steal secrets using a variety of advanced methods.

Espionage has always been an issue, but with the advances in science and technology, it is likely that it will become an increasingly high-tech problem in years to come.

Next Generation Science

While secret agents may still use traditional espionage methods, in the future, cyberespionage will become increasingly important. That means that many of the world's best computer scientists will be needed to develop new methods of protection against cyberattacks. It is likely that countries will also actively seek out the world's most devious hackers to help them launch secret cyberattacks against their rivals. Where once countries relied on spies living undercover around the world, in the future they will rely more on computer experts to find and steal the information that they need.

MAKE SPY SCIENCE YOUR FUTURE

Working in espionage and espionage investigation is both challenging and exciting. In all areas of this secretive world, sharp thinking and close attention to detail is required. If you think you have what it takes to work in this cutting-edge science field, overleaf you'll find a career guide that could one day help you stalk and stop a spy.

SPY-STOPPING CAREERS

COULD YOU STALK A SPY?

Spy dramas win record viewings, and these gripping shows have inspired many to enter the world of espionage and counterintelligence. It is an amazingly exciting field to work in, with new, game-changing developments emerging all the time.

Working in counterintelligence is incredibly varied—from computer forensics to cryptography and toxicology, there are many specialties. Let's take a look at some of the exciting areas of work in the charts featured below.

Working for the FBI

- Special agent: conducting national security investigations

- Cryptanalyst: cracking codes

- Toxicologist: examining **samples** for poisons and drugs

- Surveillance specialist: performing physical surveillance operations

- IT specialist: protecting against cyberattacks and digital espionage

Working for the US Army and Other Organizations

There are many roles to be found in the US Army and other organizations that are similar to those in the FBI chart shown left, so recruitment is not limited to the FBI. Private companies require similar skills but may not require security clearance.

To pursue a career in counterintelligence, follow this simple flowchart.

Focus on STEM subjects at school
▼

Science subjects are particularly important for future careers in counterintelligence.

Choose a career area to specialize in
▼

There are many skills required for different jobs in the security industry, so now is a good time to decide what you want to do.

Earn a bachelor's degree
▼

A bachelor's degree is a requirement for most jobs in the industry, especially to work in the FBI or US Army. Pick a degree relevant to your chosen speciality, such as math, computer science, forensics, or psychology.

Enrol on an **internship** program
▼

The FBI offers an internship program for undergraduates, but requires a GPA of 3.0 or over.

Consider additional study and training
▼

Depending on the job you are interested in, additional training or study may be required. This may be a master's degree or doctorate, or a specialized course offered by the organization that you wish to work for.

Apply for Jobs

Some roles require additional experience, so you may need to work in another role until you have the experience to apply for your chosen area.

GLOSSARY

analyzed carefully studied something in order to better understand it

biological warfare warfare involving the use of biological weapons

Cold War a period of increased suspicion and hostility between the West and Russia that lasted from the end of World War II until the early 1990s

commissioned ordered to go ahead

confidential containing information that only certain people are allowed to see

deciphering figuring out the meaning of secret messages

deflecting turning away from its intended course

embassies government offices abroad

emits gives off

encryption the art of turning something into secret code

foiling stopping a plan

hacked gained access to a computer or computer network for illegal purposes

hostile not friendly

illegal against the law

intelligence information concerning an enemy or potential enemy

intercepting getting hold of, seeing, or hearing something before it reaches its intended target

internship gaining practical, usually unpaid, work experience within an organization

legal within the law

location the place where something is found

malicious harmful

monitoring checking or keeping watch over

operatives undercover agents

orbiting moving around a planet

pandemic an outbreak of a disease that occurs over a wide geographic area, such as multiple countries or continents, and typically affects a significant proportion of the population

permission the act of allowing someone to do something

personnel people who work for an organization

radar a system used to send and receive signals or messages using radio waves, usually with the purpose of locating a particular object

rivals one or more people, organizations, or countries that are trying to gain the same thing

rogue something or someone who operates outside of accepted boundaries

samples small parts of something taken to examine them scientifically

satellites man-made devices sent into space for specific purposes

security the safety of a country, organization, or person

software computer programs that tell a computer what to do

stability safe and in balance

suspects people suspected of carrying out crimes

terrorism the use of terror to make a person, organization, or country do something

virtual describes a world that is created by computers